Oh, Behave!

Manners at School

Siân Smith

Chicago, Illinois

www.capstonepub.com
Visit our website to find out
more information about
Heinemann-Raintree books.

To order:
☎ Phone 800-747-4992
🖥 Visit www.capstonepub.com
to browse our catalog and order online.

© 2013 Raintree
an imprint of Capstone Global Library, LLC
Chicago, Illinois

Edited by Dan Nunn, Rebecca Rissman, and John-Paul Wilkins
Designed by Marcus Bell
Picture research by Elizabeth Alexander
Production by Alison Parsons
Originated by Capstone Global Library Ltd
Printed and bound in China by Leo Paper Products Ltd

16 15 14 13 12
10 9 8 7 6 5 4 3 2 1

Library of Congress Cataloging-in-Publication Data
Smith, Siân.
  Manners at school / Siân Smith.
     pages cm.—(Oh, behave!)
  Includes bibliographical references and index.
  ISBN 978-1-4329-6637-9 (hb)—ISBN 978-1-4329-6642-3 (pb)
1. Etiquette for children and teenagers. 2. Elementary schools—
Juvenile literature. I. Title.
  BJ1857.C5S63 2012
  395.5—dc23   2011049831

Acknowledgments
We would like to thank the following for permission to reproduce
photographs: © Capstone Publishers pp. 7, 15, 16, 17, 22 (Karon
Dubke); © Corbis p. 8; Alamy p. 19 (© Bubbles Photolibrary);
Corbis pp. 9, 23 (© Tomas Rodriguez); Getty Images pp. 4
(Rayes/Digital Vision), 6 (Jonathan Kirn/Riser), 11, 22 (Floresco
Productions/Cultura), 13, 22 (Rubberball/Nicole Hill), 21
(Superstudio/The Image Bank); iStockphoto pp. 14, 22 (©
Christopher Futcher), 23 (© Julia Savchenko); Shutterstock pp. 5,
23 (© Darrin Henry), 10, 12, 18, 20 (© Monkey Business Images).

Front cover photograph of schoolgirls making faces reproduced
with permission of Shutterstock (© StockLite). Rear cover
photograph of three children reading together reproduced with
permission of Shutterstock (© Darrin Henry).

Every effort has been made to contact copyright holders
of material reproduced in this book. Any omissions will be
rectified in subsequent printings if notice is given to the
publisher.

We would like to thank Nancy Harris and Dee Reid for their
assistance in the preparation of this book.

Contents

Good Manners

People with good manners know how to behave in different places.

If you have good manners, people will enjoy having you at school.

At School

Hold doors open for other people.

Don't shut the door without looking.

Move quietly around school.

If you are noisy, you will disturb people.

In Class

Listen to the person who is talking.

Don't talk when you should be listening.

Say "please" and "thank you" when
you ask for help.

Don't fool around or upset people.

Wait for your turn.

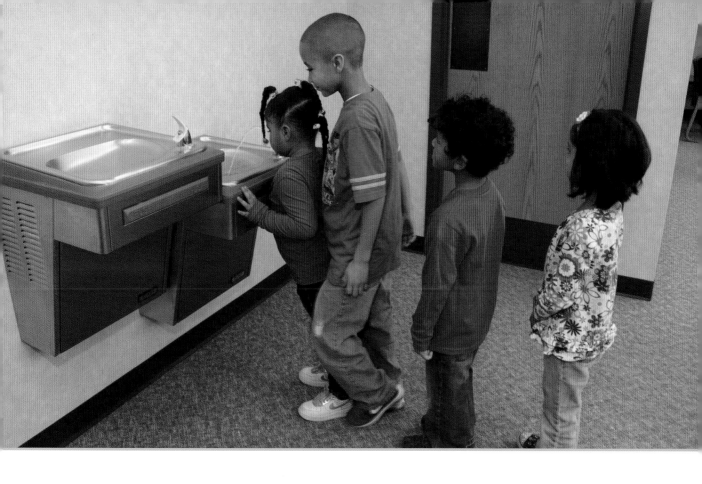

Don't push in front of other people.

Ask if you need to borrow something.

Don't take other people's things.

On the Playground

Ask people if they would like to play.

Don't leave people out of
your games.

All the Time

Say nice things when you are with other people.

Treat people the way you like to
be treated.

Best Behavior

Who here has good manners?

Answer on page 24

Picture Glossary

borrow to use something that belongs to someone else

disturb do something that stops people from doing what they need to do

good manners ways of behaving politely and well

Index

Answer to question on page 22
The children with their hands up waiting for the teacher have good manners.

Notes for parents and teachers
Before reading
Explain that good manners are ways of behaving—they help us to understand what to do and how to act. They are important because they show us how to treat each other and help us to get along well with other people. What examples of good manners can the children think of? List these together.

After reading
- What manners do the children think are important in school? Agree on a class list of the most important ones together. Phrase each manner in a positive way (for example "ask if you can borrow things" rather than "don't grab"). Create a book of these good manners. Children can take photographs of the manners being shown in class to illustrate the book.
- Play a manners drawing game. Draw some pictures on the board that show manners at school. Ask the children to guess what is being shown. Role-playing could be used instead of drawing, if the manners are harder to demonstrate through drawings.